90-43

578   Stwertka, Eve
STW   Microscope

11A8459

$9.98

DATE			
OCT 2 1990			
SEP. 1 5 1992			
SEP. 2 2 1992			
SEP. 1 5 1993			
SEP 2 6 1995			

© THE BAKER & TAYLOR CO.

MICROSCOPE

Also by
Eve and
Albert Stwertka

MAKE IT GRAPHIC!
Drawing Graphs
for Science and
Social Studies
Projects

MICROSCOPE

HOW TO USE IT
AND ENJOY IT

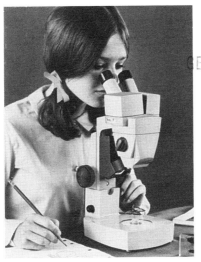

EVE AND ALBERT STWERTKA

JULIAN MESSNER

JULIAN MESSNER and colophon are trademarks
of Simon & Schuster, Inc. Design by Raul Rodriguez.
Manufactured in the United States of America.

Photo credits: Reichert-Jung, Inc.— Cambridge
Instruments Co. t.p., Hugh Spencer from National
Audubon p. 7, Carolina Biological Supply Co.
pp. 27, 42, 61, 63.

(Lib. ed.) 10 9 8 7 6 5 4 3 2 1
(Paper ed.) 10 9 8 7 6 5 4 3 2 1

Library of Congress Cataloging-in-Publication Data

Stwertka, Eve.
  Microscope: how to use it and enjoy it.

  Includes index.
  Summary: Discusses the development and opera-
tion of microscopes, how to make slides, and the
technique to use in studying them.
  1. Microscope   and   microscopy—Juvenile
literature.   2. Microscope and microscopy—Technique—Juvenile literature. [1. Microscope and mi-
croscopy] I. Stwertka, Albert. II. Title.
QH278.S79 1988   578   88-23127
ISBN 0-671-63705-3
ISBN 0-671-67060-3 (pbk.)

The authors' sincere thanks go to Mel
Sobel Microscopes, Ltd., of Hicksville,
Long Island, for help and encourage-
ment, and also to Ruth K. Fisher of the
City University of New York for her expert
suggestions.

CONTENTS

1

WORLDS
INSIDE A SPECK

A microscope is your window on a secret world. It shows you things that are usually invisible because they are too small for your bare eyes to see. The microscope makes everything look bigger. We say it *magnifies* the appearance of things. It can make a thread look as thick as a rope, change an insect leg into a giant claw, and turn a drop of water into an aquarium of strange swimming creatures.

The name *microscope* comes from *micro,* meaning small, and *scope,* an instrument for viewing things. Before the microscope was developed, no one knew about the unseen universe of tiny structures we now call the *microcosm.* For thousands of years people thought there was nothing smaller than the smallest things they could see around them. No one knew that a speck of earth or a drop of water could contain beautiful and complicated forms.

Then the art of making transparent glass was developed. People soon noticed that when they peered at an object through a glass ball or bead, the object looked larger. By grinding and polishing the glass they could shape it into a lens that would bring out just the right enlarging effect.

About seven hundred years ago lens makers already knew how to make spectacles to help people see more clearly. Of course, these spectacles didn't quite look like ours today. The lenses were small and imperfect, because even the best glass at that time was greenish and full of little air bubbles.

By the seventeenth century, though, lenses had been much improved. It was a time when people were very curious about their surroundings. Finding out how nature worked was a great new adventure. The age of science had begun. In England, a group of people founded the Royal Society for the Promotion of Natural Knowledge. One of its members was Robert Hooke, an Englishman born in 1635, who became one of the great investigators in scientific history.

ROBERT HOOKE'S MICROSCOPES

While other great naturalists of his day were fitting glass lenses into telescopes for gazing at distant objects in the sky, Robert Hooke was busy devising microscopes for looking at small objects close at hand. In fact, Hooke's microscopes looked rather like telescopes. They consisted of two lenses at opposite ends of a long tube attached to a stand.

When Hooke prepared to examine a plant or an insect, he would stick it on a pin mounted in front of the lower lens of his microscope. At first he had to work in the sun, because only sunlight was bright enough to show him his object clearly. Eventually, though, he added a flaming oil lamp and a mirror to the microscope assembly. The mirror concentrated the light of the

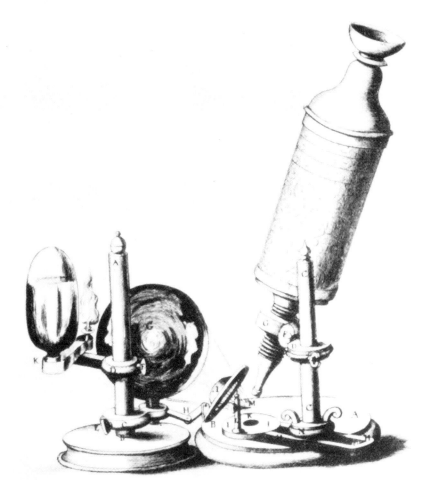

Robert Hooke published this drawing of his microscope in 1665.

lamp and cast it over the specimen. Ever since, mirrors have been standard equipment on microscopes.

Curious about everything around him, Robert Hooke looked at mosses, molds, crystals, cork, the head of a fly, and the muscles and tendons of small animals. Hooke was the first person to record

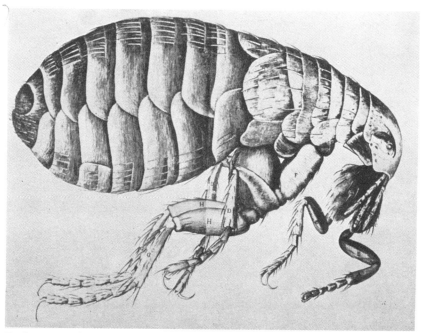

Robert Hooke's famous drawing of a magnified flea. His original illustration is about 16 inches long.

that a leaf is actually made of small rectangular cells arranged like bricks. He was also the first to observe the perfect crystal structure of a snowflake that he managed to catch on a black cloth.

Robert Hooke made careful drawings of everything he saw under the microscope. His most famous picture caused quite a sensation. It was a closeup of a flea, enlarged to nearly 16 inches in length. He reported his findings at weekly meetings of the Royal Society, where his fellow members wanted to see more and more of his demonstrations. They made him Curator of Experiments and charged him with taking them on a new adventure in microscopy at each of their weekly meetings.

LEEUWENHOEK'S LENSES

Robert Hooke devoted himself to magnifying parts of visible, familiar things. He didn't suspect that on a still smaller scale there existed forms of life that were as yet invisible and unknown. This discovery belongs to Hooke's contemporary, Anthony van Leeuwenhoek, born in Holland in 1632.

Leeuwenhoek was a successful linen merchant. In his business he had to look closely at many types of cloth fibers, which may have led to his passion for exploring the hidden universe of tiny objects. Making lenses was his hobby, and since he lived to the age of ninety-one, he had many years to perfect his skill. He was able to grind small beads of glass or clear quartz crystal

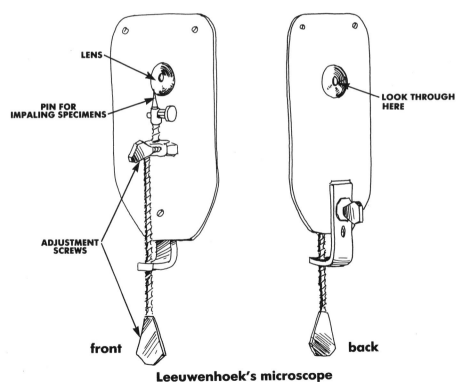

LENS

PIN FOR
IMPALING SPECIMENS

LOOK THROUGH
HERE

ADJUSTMENT
SCREWS

front　　　　　　　　**back**

Leeuwenhoek's microscope

into magnifiers so powerful that experts now estimate his best instruments must have enlarged things about three hundred times.

Leeuwenhoek's microscopes looked different from Hooke's. While Hooke used two lenses, one at each end of a long tube, Leeuwenhoek fastened a single bead-like lens into a flat metal holder. Both instruments were imitated and became about equally popular for many years. Both presented difficulties, though. In Hooke's compound microscope, the double lenses and the long, dark tube caused distortions and lighting problems. On the other hand, Leeuwenhoek's simple microscope was hand-held and tiring to use. Some time around 1830, when glass making and lens grinding were perfected, the compound microscope with its two lenses won out as the definitive model.

LITTLE GREEN ANIMALS

Leeuwenhoek never tired of training his microscope on every object and substance that came his way. Late one summer, he went boating on a lake whose waters turned cloudy just at that season every year. The natives thought that this was caused by the heavy dew. But Leeuwenhoek took a vial of the water home with him and looked at it through his microscope.

To his amazement he found the water to be swarming with little animals. In a famous letter to the Royal Society he described the various "animalcules." Some of these were green, some white, others transparent or ashy grey. One kind was oval shaped, with two tiny limbs near the head and two little fins at the rear of the body. He estimated that these creatures must be about a thousand times smaller than the smallest mites he had seen on cheese rind or in infested flour.

MEDICINE AND THE MICROSCOPE

Here was a fabulous discovery, although the impact on human

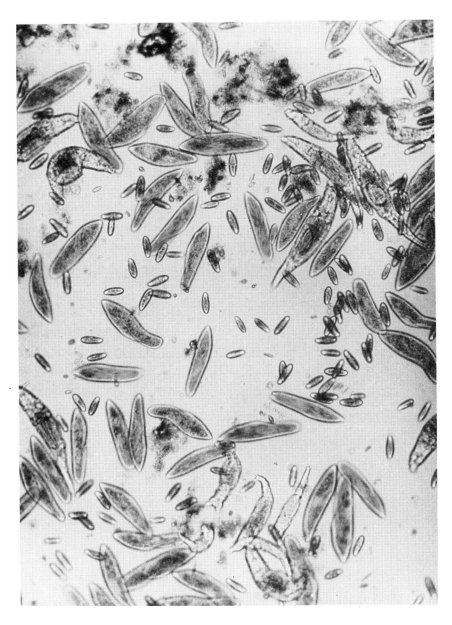

Protozoa in a drop of water magnified under a microscope.

life of all these "little animals" was not yet clear to anyone. Today we know that myriads of different microorganisms exist. Though some are dangerous and can make us very sick, others are quite harmless and still others are highly useful to us. Being able to examine microbes closely under the microscope has enabled scientists to find preventives and cures for many diseases.

THE SCIENCE OF ANATOMY

The newly developed microscope was an important tool in helping scientists discover how the human body is structured and how it works. One of the earliest of the great anatomists was the Italian, Marcello Malpighi (1628–1694). It was his practice to open animals alive so that he could observe the functioning internal organs under the microscope. In his experiments with frogs, he was the first to see the blood coursing through a network of small tubes on the surface of the lungs. This confirmed the existence of *capillaries,* small blood vessels that link veins and arteries, at a time when doctors still had an imperfect understanding of the circulatory system.

In the nineteenth century, the rapid advance of medical knowledge was partly due to the microscope. Without it, how could doctors and surgeons have discovered the structure of internal organs, the complex tissues of bone or skin, or the red and white cells of blood? Trying to imagine how these things could have been done without the microscope helps us realize the full importance of this wonderful instrument.

2

WHY THINGS LOOK LARGER

As you know, objects always look bigger when they are closer. To check the fine details on a postage stamp, for example, you are likely to bring it as close to your eyes as possible. As it comes nearer it looks larger. But there is a limit to how near you can bring it. If the stamp is too close, the eye can no longer focus on it, and the stamp looks blurred. To overcome this handicap we need to add artificial lenses. This is the job of the microscope. It permits us to bring objects as close to our eyes as we like.

BENDING THE LIGHT

The microscope does its job by using lenses to bend and change the direction of light waves. A lens can bend, or *refract*, light because light slows when it travels through glass. Have you ever noticed that a spoon looks bent when it is half-immersed in water?

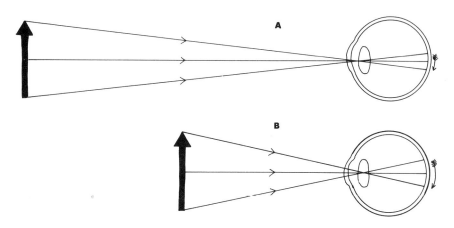

An object that is far away creates a small image in the eye (A). When you bring it closer (B), it creates a bigger image.

The light ray leaving the spoon bends as it passes from the water into the air, because light travels more slowly in water than in air. The same is true of glass.

THE SIMPLE MICROSCOPE

The simplest microscope consists of a single lens, one that is thicker at the center than at the edges. This lens changes the direction of light passing through it so that it stops spreading out and *converges* again to form an image of the source.

It's easy to understand how a lens can form an image. Think of a light wave from a distant source approaching the lens. The light wave is very much like the ocean wave you would see at the beach when a breaker rolls toward the shore. As the center of the wave starts to pass through the thick part of the lens, the two ends of the wave are still traveling through the air. Since light travels more slowly in glass than in air, the center of the

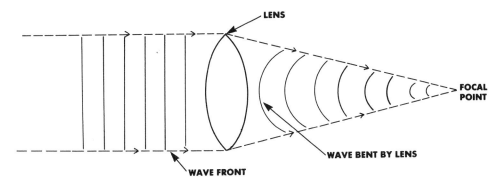

LENS

FOCAL POINT

WAVE BENT BY LENS

WAVE FRONT

When the wave front passes through the lens, the center slows down and the light is bent.

wave slows down, while the two ends keep on going at their original speed. What happens, then, is that the wave is bent around by the lens and emerges from the other side curved like the letter C. This newly shaped wave will form ever-tighter circles as it proceeds through the air, until it finally converges to a single point. This point, where the image forms, is called the *focal point* of the lens. The distance from the lens to the focal point is called the *focal length*. The shorter the focal length, the greater the power of the lens to take a wave form and bend it around so that it will converge.

Sometimes, however, the lens doesn't have enough power to converge the light. This happens when the source is very close to the lens. In that case the image formed by the lens does not appear on the viewer's side, but rather in back of the lens on the same side as its source. As you look through the lens you see the image on the far side, enlarged and more distant. The simple microscope works on this principle. By adjusting the position of the object with respect to the lens, you can get the largest image that you can see without straining your eyes.

The Compound Microscope

A microscope with a single lens, the so-called simple microscope, is, in fact, nothing more than a magnifying glass. Today, most microscopes use two lenses for greater magnification. These compound microscopes feature an upper lens—the eyepiece, or *ocular* lens—and a lower lens, at the opposite end of a tube—the *objective* lens.

First, a magnified image is formed by the objective lens, and projected up into the tube. This image is upside down. Next, the eyepiece takes over and enlarges the image once again, still leaving it upside down. As a result, what you see in a microscope is always reversed. For example, when you move the object up, the image appears to move down. When you move it to the right, the image appears to move to the left.

The magnifying powers of the objective and the eyepiece are usually marked on the casing of the lenses. A typical medium-power objective has a magnification of about 40×, which means that it magnifies the object 40 times. The magnification of the eyepiece is usually 12.5×. You can easily figure out the total magnification of your microscope. Remember that what you are looking at has been magnified twice, first by the objective and then by the eyepiece. To obtain the total, multiply the two magnifying powers. If the objective is marked 40× and the eyepiece 12.5×, then the total magnification is 500×, or 40 × 12.5.

Depth of Focus

One of the first things you will notice when you examine an object with any thickness is that under the microscope only a very thin single layer of the object seems to be in focus. At high degrees of magnification, the distance of the object from the objective is very important. Even a tiny change in this distance causes a major change in the position of the image. The result is that only a tiny slice of the object is ever in focus at any one time. The greater the magnification, the smaller this *depth of focus.*

The microscope has other limitations. Only specimens that are transparent or reflect a great deal of light can be clearly seen. Most specimens are cut into very thin slices before they are placed under the lens. If this is impractical, there are other ways to prepare a great number and variety of things so that they can be successfully examined.

Chromatic Aberration

Many lenses have an important flaw that affects their usefulness. Although the light from the sun or a lightbulb looks white, it is really made up of various colors. Each color travels through glass at a different speed, and therefore each color has its own focal length. When lenses don't correct for this, the images they form tend to be blurred and ringed with colors. This defect is known as *chromatic aberration.* It can be greatly reduced by combining lenses made of different types of glass. These *achromatic lenses* are an important feature to look for when buying a microscope.

3

HANDLING
THE MICROSCOPE

Like any delicate scientific instrument, the microscope must be handled with skill and care. A few simple precautions can make all the difference between success and frustration.

Set up your microscope on a large, steady table. There should be enough space to hold samples, slides, chemicals, and a notebook in which you can write and draw—all the equipment you need for your work.

Remove the microscope carefully from its case. Always carry it by putting one hand under the horseshoe-shaped base and grasping the curved stand that supports the tube and its lenses with the other hand. Everything should be in working order, clean and free of dust. If you have a slide with a prepared sample, place it on the stage of the microscope. A cover slip should always be on top of the slide. There are usually spring clips to hold the

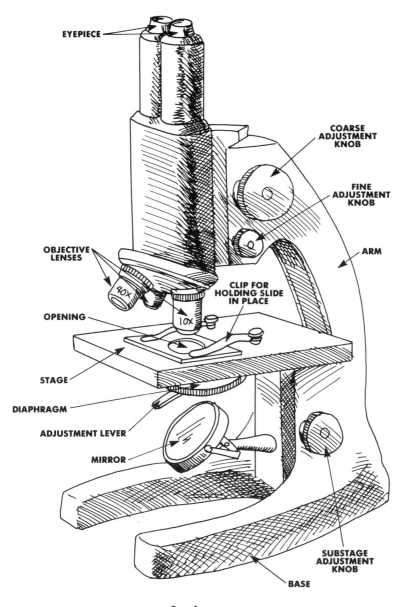

EYEPIECE

COARSE
ADJUSTMENT
KNOB

FINE
ADJUSTMENT
KNOB

ARM

OBJECTIVE
LENSES

40X

10X

CLIP FOR
HOLDING SLIDE
IN PLACE

OPENING

STAGE

DIAPHRAGM

ADJUSTMENT LEVER

MIRROR

SUBSTAGE
ADJUSTMENT
KNOB

BASE

A microscope

slide in place. Make sure that the specimen to be observed is directly over the hole in the stage.

SOURCES OF LIGHT

Daylight is generally not your best source of light. A passing cloud can force you to interrupt your work at any time. Nor should you ever work in direct sunlight. To do so is quite dangerous, because the microscope can focus sunlight to such a high intensity that it can damage your eyes. Besides, sunlight can damage parts of the microscope and destroy your specimen.

The best source of light is an ordinary electric lamp with a strong, unfrosted lightbulb. Place it on the table next to the microscope. Most microscopes contain a movable mirror located below the stage to help concentrate the light by reflecting it up through the sample. The mirror usually has two sides. One side is flat, and the other side is concave like the inside of a bowl. The concave mirror is designed to be used with high-power magnification. It is best to try both sides and use the one that gives you the most even background illumination and the clearest image. After you position the lamp so that the light strikes the center of the mirror, adjust the mirror to direct the light upward into the microscope.

Some microscopes are equipped with a *diaphragm*—a plate that limits the size of the opening—under the stage. This controls the amount of light that reaches the specimen and can make looking at transparent samples much more comfortable. Besides, different lighting sometimes brings out different details in your sample. By moving a small lever on the side, you can regulate the size of the opening in the diaphragm and increase or decrease the light intensity.

THE OBJECTIVES

Most microscopes have two or three objectives mounted on a

revolving nosepiece attached to the bottom of the main tube. You can change the magnification by turning from one objective to another. Sometimes the objectives can even be unscrewed from their mounts and replaced with different sizes. The choice of objectives on the revolving turret usually provides low, medium, and high magnification. The magnifying power is engraved on each objective. A fairly typical set of objectives might consist of three lenses whose magnifications are 10×, 40×, and 100×.

Always start by using the objective with the lowest power. You can see a larger area of your specimen with the low-power lens. This enables you to select the part you will want to examine in greater detail. Low magnification also gives you a greater depth of focus, so you get a clearer initial view of the specimen. Be careful not to touch any of the glass parts as you handle the nosepiece. Fingerprints not only distort the image but also can damage the lens.

SCANNING YOUR SPECIMEN

Now look at the objective from the side and turn the coarse adjustment, usually the larger of the two thumbscrews, until the front lens of the objective is just above the slide. Using the coarse adjustment screw, slowly raise the tube until an image comes into view. At first the image will be blurred. Carefully move the tube up and down until you get the clearest image.

To make sure the part of the specimen you want to examine is precisely over the hole in the stage, you may have to move the slide. Some microscopes have an adjustment screw that moves the stage backwards and forwards as well as from side to side.

Always remember to raise the tube until the image appears. If you begin by lowering the tube, you might accidentally push the objective into the slide. This might damage the objective lens or crush the specimen. Once the image is in view, you can perfect your adjustment by turning the fine adjustment knob.

CHANGING MAGNIFICATION

When you want to go on to a higher magnification, carefully swing the new objective into position by rotating the nosepiece. The higher power lens will be longer than the low-power lens, so be careful not to hit the slide as you rotate it into position. Always check this carefully by looking at the lens from the side. If you find that there isn't enough clearance for the new objective, raise the tube and start the whole focusing process over again.

With a higher power objective your field of view is much smaller, so you won't see as much of the specimen. You may have to move the slide carefully around the stage until the part that interests you is again in view. You will also find that the depth of focus is much narrower, so you will constantly have to operate the fine focusing mechanism. Each turn of the knob will bring a different layer of the specimen into sharp focus.

Experienced microscopists hardly ever stop using the fine adjustment. They find that this cuts down on eyestrain and allows them to see every part of the specimen.

Do not make the mistake of assuming that the bigger the magnification the better. With extremely high magnification you can see only a small part of your specimen. The image is usually very dim, and many details are no longer clearly defined.

VISUAL STATIC

As you move the slide from side to side, you'll notice that the motion of the image is just the reverse of yours. When you move the slide to the right, the image shifts to the left. When you move the slide up, the image moves down. The reason for this, of course, as we saw in Chapter 2, is that a microscope produces an *inverted* image, with all the directions reversed. It takes practice to move the slide efficiently so you can quickly get any part of the specimen into view.

Avoiding Eyestrain

Scientists who constantly work with microscopes find that they suffer much less eyestrain if they keep both eyes open while looking into the microscope. Although the natural tendency might be to close your free eye, you should practice working with both eyes open.

If you wear eyeglasses, you may wonder whether you should wear them while looking into the microscope. It's generally better to work without glasses. You can usually make the necessary adjustments through the optics of the microscope. If you must use glasses, prevent scratching them by putting specially designed rubber guards on the eyepiece of the microscope.

Every so often, tiny threads or specks may seem to float in front of your eyes while you are observing a specimen. Don't be alarmed. These so-called floaters are often a result of eyestrain, and everyone has them to some extent. They are produced in the fluid of the eye, and they usually disappear fairly rapidly.

Caring for Your Microscope

To get good results with your microscope, maintain it in good condition. Guard it from dust. Cover it with a plastic hood when you're not using it, and always store it in its case. Clean it very carefully to prevent scratching the lenses. If some of the lenses have fingerprints, clean them either with lens paper or with some alcohol and a cotton swab. Cleaning the microscope often will prolong its life and save you the time and expense of a major overhaul.

4

ADVENTURES CLOSE TO HOME

Look around and you'll find an abundance of things to examine under the microscope. It's best to start with a few specimens that are easy to obtain and to prepare. A good way to practice focusing is to concentrate on a single letter in a printed document. Start by cutting a horizontal strip from a newspaper page. Then pick a letter located near the center and draw a ring around it. Keep in mind that when you locate this letter through the microscope you'll be seeing it upside down and backwards. To avoid confusion, pick a letter that shows this clearly—an "a" or an "e" will be fine.

MOUNTING A SLIDE

A strip of newspaper can easily be placed under the microscope and examined without any further preparation. But very few other

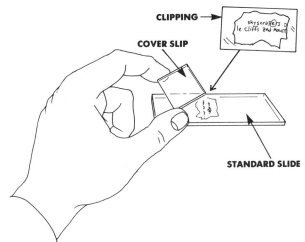

CLIPPING →

COVER SLIP

skyscrap(e)rs of
le cliffs and mount

STANDARD SLIDE

To mount a newspaper clipping, place it on a slide, put a drop of water on it to keep it from slipping off, and top it with a cover slip.

Under the microscope, the letter "e" appears upside down. The rough texture of the newspaper fibers can be clearly seen.

specimens will be so simple to get ready. Some of the things you might want to look at will be small as well as fragile, and many will come in liquid form. To make them easier to handle, they must be mounted on a slide and topped by a cover slip.

A standard microscope slide is a glass rectangle, 3 inches long and 1 inch wide. The cover slip is an extremely thin glass plate which may be square or circular. It holds the sample in place and protects it. Both slides and cover glasses are obtainable at small cost from microscope dealers and biological supply houses.

Let's use the letter you circled on the newspaper page to make your first slide mount. Cut the area around the letter to a small square. Place it in the center of the slide and gently drop a cover glass on top of it to hold it in place. Always hold slides and slips by the edges to avoid getting fingerprints on them, but take care you don't cut yourself.

The cover slip will not adhere to the dry newspaper, and if you tilt the stage of your microscope it will slide off. One way to make it stick for a few moments is by placing a drop of water on the paper. If you want to make your mount semipermanent, though, use a drop of clear white corn syrup instead of water. It might be a good idea to keep this mount as a test slide to help you focus in the future.

Now slip the finished slide under the two clips on the stage of the microscope, making sure the circled letter is centered over the opening so that light can shine through the sample from below.

As we mentioned in Chapter 3, adjusting the light, locating your target, and focusing are all a bit tricky. "Focusing up" is the most important item to remember. Watch from the side as you bring your microscope tube down. Then look through the ocular and focus by bringing the tube up toward you. Move the slide left, and watch the image move right. Move the slide up, and watch the image move down. Take a good look at your letter when you have it well in focus. Remembering its topsy-turvy appearance may help you understand what you are seeing when you focus on other, more complex specimens.

PERMANENT SLIDE MOUNTS

Looking through the microscope, you may see something so striking that you wish to show it to others or study it again later. You may also wish to have a series of slides to record the changes in some plant at different seasons, or you may want to collect slides of different parts of some insect. In fact, a slide library might come in handy as a hobby or school project.

Not all specimens lend themselves equally well to being preserved. Insect parts, for example, work very well, because they are fairly dry and solid. Experiment a bit to get good results.

Place your specimen on the slide, add a few drops of a product named Euparal, and top this with a cover glass. Euparal, a neutral mounting material that can be thinned with ordinary isopropyl alcohol, hardens into a colorless, transparent, glasslike substance. It can be ordered from any chemical supply house. (You will find a list of suppliers at the end of this book.)

The finished slide will harden more quickly if you let it dry in a warm place. One way to do this is to place the slide on your work table and bend a gooseneck lamp fairly close to it. Allow the bulb to warm the slide for several hours until it hardens.

Other mounting agents are also on the market, such as Canada balsam, Permount, and Clearmount. These are more difficult to work with, because the specimen to be mounted must be completely dry. What recommends them even less is that they have to be used with chemical solvents that are flammable and harmful if inhaled.

Permanent mounts can last for many years. Before you store your collection, paste a label on each slide or mark it with a wax-tipped pencil. Record the name of the specimen, the date, and the stain, if any, used in the preparation. You can number the slides or keep an alphabetical list to help you find what you are looking for.

You may also wish to supplement your own slide collection with ready-made slides from a biological supplier. Possibilities range from a variety of insect parts to plant tissue, bacteria, and cells from various organs of the body.

FIBERS AND FABRICS

Let's return to the letter from a newspaper you mounted on a slide. Now that you see it magnified, its sharp black outlines probably look more like inky smudges. This effect is partly due to the coarse, bumpy texture of the paper. Inexpensive paper of the kind called newsprint is made of pressed wood pulp. Look for bits of individual wood fibers. They are pitted and spiraled, showing that they were once live cells of trees. By comparison, fine stationery made of linen fiber is far more even textured. Cigarette paper, which is made of rice straw, is thin but strong and close-textured to make it slow in burning. To compare the textures of different kinds of paper, cut out squares and mount them. Try paper towels, napkins, and tissues. Keep a record and write a short description of the qualities of each.

Paper is manufactured from a mash of short fibers, then dried over sieves and rolled flat. Certain textile fabrics are made in a similar way. Felt, for example, is a strong, water-resistant fabric of matted, pressed wool used to make hats and slippers. Most other fabrics, though, are likely to be knitted or woven.

Any knitted garment, whether factory knit or handmade, is composed of a long, continuous filament, or thread, looped together in interlocking rows. Most underwear and stockings are made this way. A woven fabric, on the other hand, consists of two sets of threads. One set runs lengthwise (the warp), and the other from side to side (the woof). This basic formula allows for hundreds of different patterns and textures.

Look at several kinds of textiles. If you can't cut and mount a square of a certain fabric, try spreading it right across the stage of the microscope. Examine a fine cotton handkerchief, a T-shirt,

In this woven linen handkerchief, the fibers interlace at right angles to each other.

In this knitted cotton T-shirt, the bundles of fibers form a chain of continuous loops.

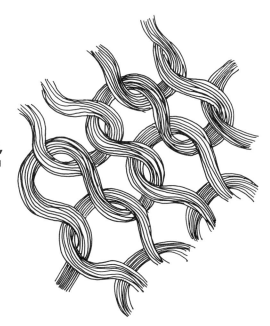

Fabrics

a nylon stocking, and a well-worn terry towel. You'll do best with materials thin enough for the light to penetrate from below the stage. If your cloth is not translucent, you'll have to rely entirely on light reflected from the surface. This will be of some interest, but it won't reveal the secrets of the texture.

If textiles appeal to you, try looking at yarns and threads, as well as unprocessed fibers such as hair and feathers. Compare cotton, silk, and nylon thread. Compare one of your own hairs to a hair from a household pet or a fur coat. In the country or in a park you're bound to find a feather dropped by a bird. Or perhaps you'll see one sticking part-way out of a down jacket or a pillow. Pull it out gently and you'll do no damage.

CRYSTALS

You don't need diamonds to see beautiful crystal structures. With a microscope, you can watch a crystal garden grow right on a glass slide. Dissolve two generous tablespoons of salt in one-quarter cup of water. Some of the salt will remain in the bottom of the cup. Place a drop of the clear liquid on a clean slide and let it spread a little. Put the slide, without a cover slip, aside for a few minutes or move it gently back and forth under a warm light bulb until the solution begins to dry. Now insert it under the microscope and focus on the outer portions of the drop.

Soon, square crystals of different sizes will form, rimmed by dark parallel lines. Salt crystals grow faster at the edges than at the center, building up steps that look like nests of open glass boxes. Move the mirror so that no light is transmitted from below, and you'll see the crystals change to gleaming three-dimensional shapes on a dark background. For crystals with a different shape, try the same experiment with boric acid instead of salt.

You can also find crystals of glittering quartz and other minerals in common sand. If you have access to a beach or a sandbox,

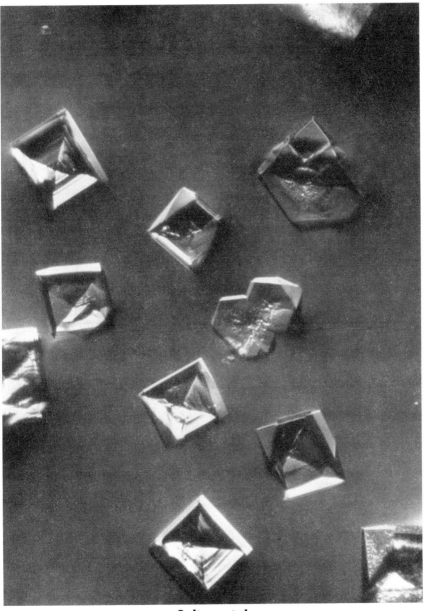

Salt crystals

take a little fine-grained sand home with you to examine close up. To view sand comfortably, keep your microscope stage horizontal to the table and omit a cover slip. The shape of sand grains can tell you something about their history. The rounder and blunter they are, the longer they are likely to have tumbled in water or wind, rubbing their edges against one another.

Occasionally, you might be surprised to find a rich sprinkling of shell fragments among the sand grains. At a few rare beaches, the stuff that looks like white sand will reveal itself under the microscope as a myriad of tiny shell pieces of delicate shapes and colors. Winds and waves have been tossing them to this fine consistency for centuries.

WET MOUNT WITH BUBBLES

To study the components of a liquid you must first spread it out thinly on a slide. This is called wet mounting. Most liquids will form a few bubbles and you should learn to recognize these, so let's begin by wet mounting something particularly bubbly. Place a small drop of a liquid laundry detergent on a slide. Using the narrow edge of a second slide, push the drop lengthwise across the first slide to spread it, then drop a cover slip gently in the center of the smear you have made. The slide should be wet only on the inside. Focus on the slide and move it back and forth. All those large and small circles with pearly centers and thick, dark outlines are air bubbles. For a test that will help you recognize them, turn your mirror aside so no bottom light reaches the slide. Under top lighting, the background liquid will look dark and the air bubbles will appear as brightly gleaming rings.

Now try another wet mount. This time, use milk. Again, you will see quite a few air bubbles. But further, your slide will be covered with small rounded shapes floating in clear liquid. These shapes are the globules of fat that give milk its white color.

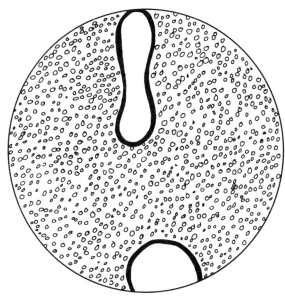

Milk magnified at 440×. The large, dark-rimmed shapes are gleaming air bubbles. The small shapes are globules of fat. Watch them drift gently in the milk.

. . . .

RECORD KEEPING AND CLEANUP

It's a good idea to keep a diary or logbook of your adventures with the microscope. First enter the date on which you made your investigation. Write down the name of the specimen you looked at and how you prepared it. Record the degree of magnification you used. Then, with a well-sharpened pencil, make a drawing of what you saw.

Cleanup is the final activity after all experiments. You won't want to face a sticky, littered table the next time you sit down to work with your microscope. Rinse dirty slides and cover glasses in liquid detergent and warm water. Lay them flat on a tissue and dry them gently with another tissue or lens paper. Keep them dust-free in a covered box. Finally, cover the microscope, and if you don't plan to use it again very soon, stow it away in its case.

. . . . . .

LIFE IN A
WATER DROP

Meet the microbes. They are the smallest forms of life, except for the organisms called viruses. Microbes are large enough to become visible under the lens of an optical microscope, but viruses are so tiny that scientists need special electronic equipment to get an image of them.

Although microbes can't be seen by the unaided eye, they often show their presence by the work or damage they can do. When bread dough rises, when apple juice turns into fizzy cider, when milk turns sour, or when a cut becomes infected, we recognize the work of microbes.

Microbes surround us and everything we touch. They even live inside our bodies. Some are helpful, others harmful. Still others don't affect us at all. Biologists have named and classified thousands of microscopic creatures and have grouped them into plant forms and animal forms. The three general groups you are likely to discover under your microscope are protozoa, bacteria, and algae.

HUNTING FOR MICROBE

Microbes need a liquid environment in order to move and reproduce. When their surroundings get dry, their bodies dry out too. They develop a hard coating and turn into inactive bits of dust. In this form some can survive for years. But as soon as they are immersed in water again they rehydrate, begin to swim around, and carry on with their life cycle.

If you want to watch microbes go about their business, you will need to give them a liquid place to live. Prepare some clean jars with screw tops to take on your microbe hunt. Good places to collect interesting specimens are stagnant puddles and ponds. Include bits of water plants and a little bottom mud in your water sample. A fish tank may also give you interesting results, and so may the water left in a vase after the flowers have faded. Collect water in several jars and label them to help you remember where each sample came from.

A REMINDER

Wash your hands thoroughly after handling water infected with microbes. Though some are harmless, others are not. While preparing slides, avoid rubbing your eyes or touching your mouth and nose. And of course, never eat while you are working with the microscope.

MICROBIAL BROTH

Another way to start a hatchery of microscopic life is to prepare a *hay infusion*. Boil two or three cups of tap water and let it stand in an open jar overnight. This gets rid of chlorine, which would destroy the growing microorganisms. Fill the jar with a handful of grass clippings, a few broken twigs, a little earth. If you can't obtain grass clippings, use wilted lettuce, carrot tops, and other vegetable refuse from the grocery store. Cover the mixture lightly so that air can get in, and put it in a warm, dark place.

After the water sample has been in the jar for 3 or 4 days, you'll probably notice that it has begun to look cloudy and smell putrid. Good. That shows the presence of microbes at work. Test a drop of the liquid under the microscope at this time, but don't be disappointed if nothing moves. More life will appear each day and, with any luck, you'll encounter quite a surprising number of organisms by the end of a week.

AQUARIUM ON A SLIDE

To give the little organisms room to swim around, use a slide with a well in it. Such slides, with a small, hollowed out depression in the center, are obtainable at stores that sell microscopes. It's easy to make your own, however. A small rubber or metal washer makes a perfect wall for a microaquarium. Glue the washer to the center of a slide with a waterproof adhesive and let it dry.

The scummier the water in the jar, the better your results are likely to be. But even if you've struck it rich in microorganisms, focusing on a water drop can be a bit tricky. Since you don't know what you might find, you don't know what to look for. The organisms appear small even though they are greatly enlarged, and most of them are nearly transparent. To make things even harder, some microbes shoot through the water too fast for clear observation, while others lie too still to be easily noticed.

To help you focus and to slow down some of the faster swimmers, lightly shred a tiny piece of paper towel or cotton. Place the fibers in the well of the slide to make a sort of thin nest. Now let a single drop of water from one of the jars fall into this nest and cover it with a cover slip. Keep the microscope level or tilt it back only slightly so the water can't run out. As usual, start with the lowest magnification and focus up. When the fibers come into view, you'll be able to tell if anything is moving around them. Sometimes cutting down the light a little will help you see things better.

The first forms of life to become visible in an infusion are likely to be bacteria. Bacteria help us, among other things, to make cheese and medicines such as penicillin. They also cause many different diseases, such as tuberculosis and infections. In appearance bacteria are small and not spectacular. Probably you'll spot them in colonies that look like rough, uneven, faintly colored patches. If you concentrate your high-focus lens on such a patch, you will be able to see a swarm of pulsating dots. Though there are hundreds of kinds of bacteria, they appear in only three general shapes. They can look like spirals, rods, or spheres.

PROTOZOA

Different environments breed different microbes. A particular water sample may contain small animals such as slow-moving worms, whirling rotifers, or minute members of the shrimp and crab family. These creatures are comparatively large, being composed of many cells. (Cells, as you will remember, are the building blocks of all living things.) But mainly, you are likely to see the single-celled organisms called protozoa.

Proto means first and *zoa* means animals. But these basic animals are not as simple as the name would lead one to believe. Nature has given their jellylike bodies many variations. With a bit of luck, you will see protozoa that are bullet-shaped, pointed, round as a ball, eel-shaped, slipper-shaped, or even trumpet-shaped.

FOUR GROUPS OF PROTOZOA

Some protozoa zoom through the water as fast as torpedoes, others hover like bees over a flower, still others jerk or hop like fleas. Biologists have divided protozoa into four classes, based on their different means of locomotion. First of all, there are the *ciliates,* which are equipped with little eyelashlike hairs (called *cilia*) that wave quickly back and forth like flexible oars. Next, we can observe the *flagellates,* which swim by means of long, whiplike tails (or *flagella*). A third group moves by sticking out projections and then letting the rest of their bodies follow. Because the projections look somewhat like shapeless feet, these protozoa are named *pseudopodia,* from the Greek roots *pseudo* and *pod,* meaning false foot. Finally, there are the *sporozoa,* which lie perfectly still after reaching their adult state because they have no

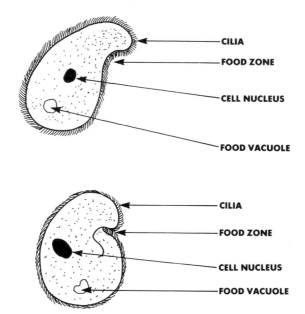

Two ciliate protozoa: *Colpidium* and *Colpoda.*

organs of locomotion. Although the sporozoa are not much fun to watch, they interest scientists because all are parasites and dangerous to larger life forms, including humans. One of the diseases caused by sporozoa is malaria.

Paramecium and Ameba

The largest and most spectacular of the ciliates you're likely to encounter in a hay infusion is the paramecium. It has an oval shape, pointed at one end, with noticeable swim hairs and an engulfing mouth like a lengthwise slit in the middle of its body. Watch its restless foraging among the smaller organisms, and observe its sizable nucleus and food-storage spaces.

In pond water, on the other hand, you will often find the best-known of the pseudopods, the ameba. When an ameba suffers a sudden jolt, such as being sucked up in an eyedropper and transferred to a slide, it becomes a perfectly still blob of jelly. But slowly it regains confidence, oozes out a footlike projection here and there, and creeps forward on its false feet. To eat, the ameba extends pseudopods, wraps them around the prey, and engulfs it whole.

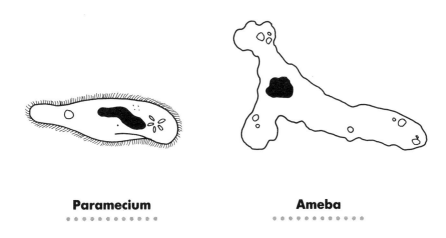

Paramecium   **Ameba**

Algae

Water from ponds or fish tanks is bound to contain many different forms of *algae*. These are simple plants without stems, roots, or leaves. They all contain *chlorophyll,* or green pigment. They range in size from single-celled forms smaller than some bacteria to seaweed many feet in length. You may find them joined together in pretty colonies forming long, bright ribbons or patterns looking like flowers. They may be green, yellow green, red, or brown.

Surprisingly, although algae are considered to be plants, some of them are energetic swimmers. You may have noticed the green scum that sometimes forms on ponds and ditches. It is caused by *Euglena,* a small, bright green, spindle-shaped organism that swims by whipping the water with its long, thin flagellum.

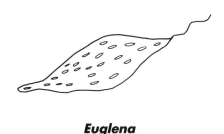

Euglena

Biologists have puzzled for a long time whether to classify *Euglena* as plant or animal. In a way it is both. Chlorophyll enables it to produce its own food. But when it has to go without light for any length of time, the green color disappears. Now the organism stays alive by absorbing ready-made nutrition in the form of decaying matter from the water, which it absorbs through its skin. While botanists (the scientists who study plants) classify *Euglena* as green algae, zoologists (the scientists who study animals) lay claim to them as flagellate protozoans.

DIATOMS

Microscopists sometimes make a hobby of collecting the charming single-celled plants called *diatoms*. Diatoms look as if they were encased in glass boxes. Their translucent shells come in a vast

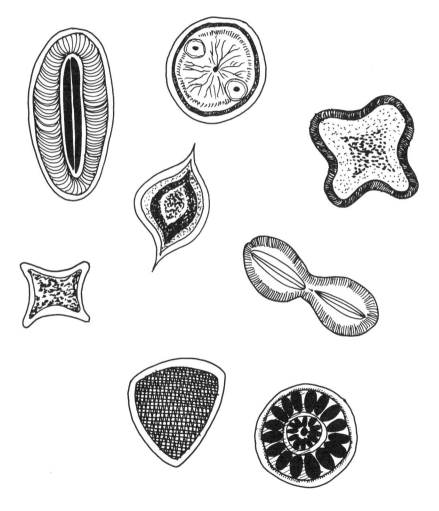

Diatoms are found in hundreds of different shapes and patterns.

variety of shapes, and some come in delicate colors. When they are magnified, they catch and reflect the light like rare and complicated jewels. In the nineteenth century, some microscopists enjoyed the painstaking hobby of collecting diatoms and arranging them on slides in samplers and patterns. One slide can hold hundreds of diatoms. Some of these intricate slides have been preserved and are valuable collectors' items today.

But diatoms are not only beautiful examples of nature's great variety of design. Deposits of these shells resulting from centuries of growth are called *diatomaceous earth*. This substance forms the basis of many commercial applications. Its scouring properties make it useful in toothpaste and fine metal polish. It also makes good commercial filters and insulating materials.

FOR BEST RESULTS

If you wish to keep a particular wet mount under the microscope for longer than half an hour or so, add a little more liquid from time to time. Do this by dipping a soft watercolor brush into the infusion and touching it to the edge of the cover glass on the slide. The water will be drawn in and merge with the moisture already there. Evaporation can be prevented by applying a small ribbon of Vaseline all around the edges of the cover glass. This is apt to be a rather messy job, but a Vaseline applicator—the kind people use on chapped lips—is helpful.

One trouble with looking at microorganisms fresh from the jar where they have been cultured is that they are mighty lively and some are too fast for comfortable observation. A nest of cotton fibers in the slide well holds them back slightly, but there are other ways to slow them down. Try placing a grain or two of yeast into the center of the slide depression. A fast, jerky swimmer like the paramecium, for example, is also a voracious eater. While paramecia are feeding on the yeast, you'll have plenty of time to observe them under higher magnification.

Another way to slow down the organisms is to let the slide dry out. As the water between the slide and the cover disappears, the cover presses down more and more tightly. You will notice protozoa becoming still in certain spots, giving you a chance to see them clearly for a while until they have dried up and disappeared.

USING STAINS FOR BETTER VISIBILITY

Professional microscopists often color slides with *stains,* or dyes, to help them see more clearly. Stains are chemicals that color parts of a specimen to enhance the contrast. They tend to concentrate in the densest parts of the specimen, making these parts appear darker. Some stains are very selective and act only on special structures within the specimen, while others color every part of it.

Many different stains can be ordered from a biological supply house. A dye such as neutral red works well for examining a water drop. It has the advantage of coloring the organisms without coloring the water. On the whole, though, ordering special chemicals may not be practical. Tincture of iodine, available at all pharmacies, is a good alternative. You can also try watercolors and food-decorating colors.

Keep in mind, though, that these work best on specimens that are not alive. Iodine is an antiseptic that kills microbes, and even watercolors and food colors will destroy the life forms in your aquarian zoo.

Chemicals that are destructive to microorganisms are not good for humans either. So always take special precautions when you work with coloring agents. Wear a pair of close-fitting rubber gloves, which you can buy at a drugstore, and make sure your work table is well protected from staining.

To convince yourself that food coloring is not as harmless as people often consider it to be, see what disaster it causes among the protozoa that live in the drop of water on your slide. Wet a small paintbrush with a little food coloring directly from the bottle. Touch the wet brush to the edge of the cover slip. As you watch through the eyepiece, you'll see the dye being slowly drawn in and diffusing through the water sample. The protozoa will slow down almost immediately in the color bath. For a moment you'll be able to focus on them very well. But within a few seconds you will see their bodies open up and dissolve into the water around them. Soon, no sign of life will remain.

LOOKING
AT PLANTS

Even the single-celled plants you can find in a drop of water come in many shapes and varieties. Larger plants, though, are built up of thousands of cells having many different functions. Under the microscope you can see the cells that make up the roots, stems, leaves, and reproductive parts of a plant.

Let's start by looking at the most eye-catching part of many plants—the flower. Gently detach one petal from a flower that grows in your home or garden. The kind and size of the flower isn't important, but a bright-colored one will give you a more beautiful sight under the microscope than a white one. Mount the petal (or a piece cut from it) between two slides. A cover slip, being thinner, would give you a better view. But it's too light to hold the petal flat and would simply fall off if you tilted your microscope stage.

Depending on the color of your petal, a dewy field of pink, gold, or blue pearls will greet your eyes. These are the cells. When the petal is fresh, its cells are plumply filled with water, making them soft and springy. Look at the slide a few days later and you'll find the cells dry and flat.

WATER DUCTS

As you know, water is essential to plants. If you forget to water your houseplants their leaves will soon go limp, and eventually they will dry out and die. How does the water you pour in the flowerpot rise from the wet soil and travel all through the plant? Under the microscope you can follow the channels it takes, from the root through the stalk to the leaves and flowers.

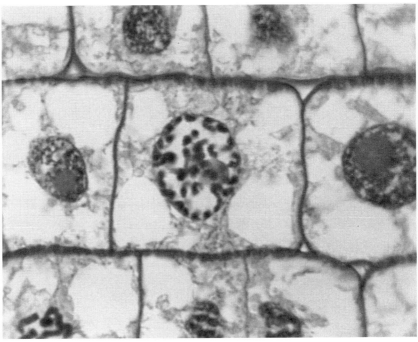

Onion root tip

No need to uproot your best potted geranium for this. Weeds and wildflowers grow everywhere, even in cities. All you have to do is carefully pull one out of the ground. It's easiest after rain, when the earth is soft. Cut samples of the plant's different parts, from the roots to the flower, and mount them on slides.

Notice the tiny root hairs trailing from the roots. This is where the water begins its journey. The root hairs are narrow tubes that search out moisture in the soil and draw it in. (The physical principle by which thin channels enable water to travel upward is called *capillary action*.)

Slice very thin cross sections of the stalk, using a single-edged razor blade and a cutproof surface. Handle the razor blade

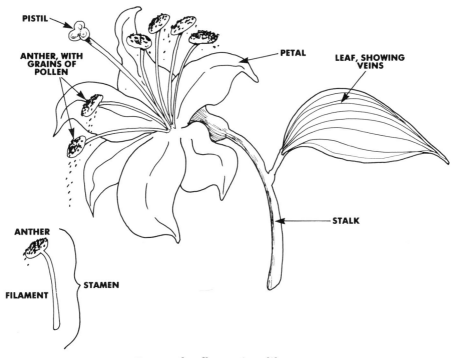

PISTIL

ANTHER, WITH GRAINS OF POLLEN

PETAL

LEAF, SHOWING VEINS

ANTHER

STAMEN

FILAMENT

STALK

Parts of a flowering lily

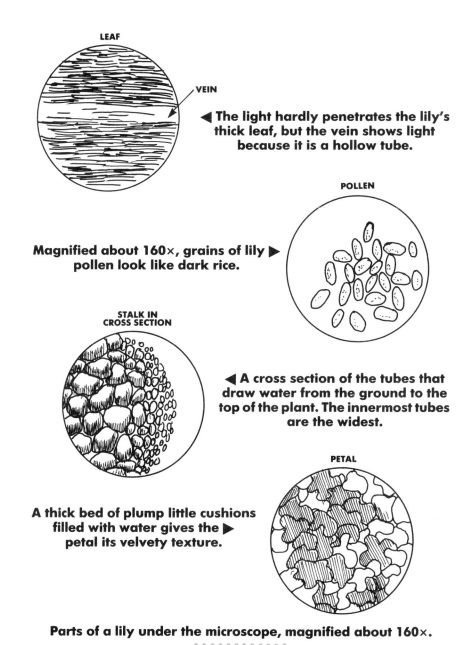

LEAF

VEIN

◀ The light hardly penetrates the lily's thick leaf, but the vein shows light because it is a hollow tube.

POLLEN

Magnified about 160×, grains of lily ▶ pollen look like dark rice.

STALK IN CROSS SECTION

◀ A cross section of the tubes that draw water from the ground to the top of the plant. The innermost tubes are the widest.

PETAL

A thick bed of plump little cushions filled with water gives the ▶ petal its velvety texture.

Parts of a lily under the microscope, magnified about 160×.

carefully to avoid cutting yourself, or ask an adult to help you. Place one or two slices on a slide without a cover slip. You'll find yourself looking straight down the bundles of tubes that bring water to the upper plant, very much like the water pipes in an apartment house. Notice the closely spaced green cells of the outer rim and the honeycomb of large, colorless cells forming the stalk's core.

Finally, prepare a slide from part of a leaf. If the leaves of your particular plant are too thick for light to shine through, use clover or some other small, thin leaf instead. The large and small veins making up the leaf's skeleton are the main waterways by which water and nutrients are carried to the cells. The rest of the plant's nourishment comes from the sun. Sunlight helps leaves to manufacture chlorophyll, the green substance you'll see stored in the carpet of tiny cells.

Pollen

Flowering plants reproduce by means of a powdery-looking substance called *pollen.* Look at the center of a mature, open flower, and you'll see its reproductive parts. The innermost projection is the *pistil,* or female sexual organ. The male organs, called the *stamens,* surround it. At the ends of the stamens you'll notice the *anthers,* baglike structures that contain the pollen. Touch the anthers and you'll find some of the pollen sticking to your finger.

Bees and other insects are attracted by the plant's bright flowers and come to drink the nectar. As they enter a flower, they come in contact with the pollen, which sticks to their legs and furry bodies. When they fly on, they carry pollen to another part of the same flower or to other flowers nearby. To produce the seed of a new plant, a pollen grain must unite with an *ovule,* or egg cell, formed in the pistil. Pollination is chiefly carried out by insects. But pollen grains are also carried to their destination

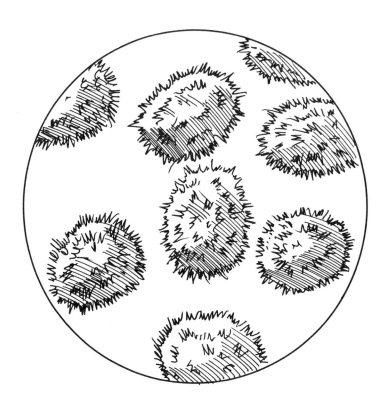

Sunflower pollen. Tiny burrs all over the surface help the grains stick wherever they land.

by the wind or by birds and animals that happen to brush against the flower.

When you examine pollen under the microscope you'll understand why it sticks to everything it touches. The surfaces of the grains are cleverly designed to make them cling. Some flower pollens have burrs, others may be ridged or spiked.

Seeds

After pollination is completed, the flower fades and the fruit, which contains the seeds, develops inside the pistil. The pit you throw away after eating a peach or cherry is nature's vehicle for making a new peach tree or cherry tree. Fruits, like flowers, attract people, birds, and animals. After the fruit has been picked and eaten, the seed is dropped. By chance, it may enter the soil and start a new plant.

Try collecting a number of different seeds. Often, you will find the new plant already curled inside a seed, waiting for the right time to emerge. Maple seeds—the ones that whirl down from the tree attached to long wings—are easy to find. But you can also use dried lentils or lima beans. Soak the dry seeds in water overnight or place them on a bed of wet cotton and wait till they start to sprout. You can open the softened seed with a needle and lay it down flat on a slide for observation.

Spores

Certain plants do not produce flowers, pollen, and seeds. Instead, they develop *spores,* which drop when they are ripe and create new plants. Mosses and ferns belong to this group of plants, and both are interesting to observe under the microscope. Ferns grow in moist, shady places and can also be found potted in stores and homes. If you turn over the *fronds,* or leaves, of a fern, you'll discover a regular pattern of brown dots on the underside. These are the cases containing the spores.

Pick a small piece of frond and place it between a slide and a cover slip. What you see depends on the time of year. In early summer, the clusters of spore cases resemble orange and brown grapes. Later, they look like thick, ropy coils of dark rings. Finally the coils open, and the closely packed brown spores begin to spill out. New plants will start where the spores fall.

The underside of a fern frond holds rows of spore cases. Below are scattered fern spores magnified at 440×.

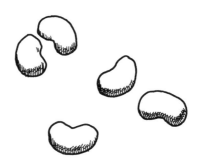

FUNGI

An even larger group of plants, the fungi, also reproduce by means of spores. Fungi don't manufacture chlorophyll, the green pigment that produces food in grass, trees, and flowering plants. Instead, fungi feed on other organisms or on decaying vegetation. Mushrooms—both edible and poisonous kinds—belong to the fungus family, and so do many types of blights, rusts, and molds.

Fungus blights destroy grains and trees and can devastate valuable food crops. Many fungi are harmless, though, and some are highly valuable. Penicillin, for example, the disease-fighting antibiotic drug, comes from a fungus belonging to the family of blue and green molds that form on leftover foods in our kitchens.

To get a magnified closeup of mold, try growing a good

To grow a mold

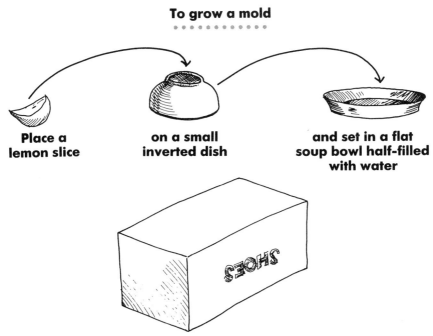

Place a lemon slice   **on a small inverted dish**   **and set in a flat soup bowl half-filled with water**

cover with an inverted shoe box and check it a week later

specimen on a lemon slice or a piece of rye bread. Cottage cheese left in the container for a few weeks will also give you good results. Molds flourish in moist, sunless places. Place a slice of lemon on a small inverted dish set in a soup bowl half-full of water. Cover this island with a jar and put it in a dark place or cover it with an inverted box. Inspect it after a few days. When the fungus has grown thick and fuzzy, scrape a little of it onto a slide with a drop of alcohol or water to plump it up for better visibility. Some molds look very much like colonies of tiny mushrooms. Others are a tangle of pale threads dotted with dark spore cases. Under high magnification you'll see the spores, which are shaped like pollen or certain seeds.

YEASTS

Let's take a look at one more group of plants in the fungus family—the yeasts. The most familiar yeast is the single-celled hidden helper that can turn sugar into alcohol and bubbly gases. Besides enabling us to make beer and wine, yeasts give us soft, springy breads and cakes.

Observing yeast cells as they go about their silent work is fascinating. One envelope of dried yeast from the store will be more than enough for your experiment. Dissolve ½ teaspoon of the yeast in 2 tablespoons of almost-hot water and add ½ teaspoon of sugar to feed the yeast cells. Stir the mixture well. Wait 10 minutes, then place a drop on a flat slide and carefully let down the cover slip on it.

At first, you will see numerous air bubbles, apparently surrounded by tiny glass beads. Nothing much will seem to be happening. Wait a few minutes longer until you notice a general streaming motion. Concentrate on the outer rim of an air bubble and switch to a higher magnification.

Now you will see the individual yeast cells, looking like millions of plump, transparent rice grains, surging and multiplying

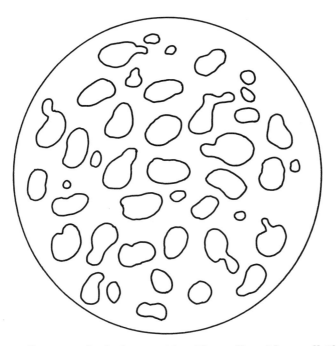

Yeast cells magnified about 600×. The cells with small "buds" are about to divide. Yeasts can be stained with a dye to make them stand out clearly.

mightily. Focus on one spot so you can observe buds forming on the parent cells, breaking off, and floating away on their own. This is how yeast cells reproduce. As the yeast works it turns the sugar in the mixture into gases. It's these gases that puff up the dough when bread is set to rise before baking. The heat of the oven kills the yeast cells. But the air spaces remain, making the bread soft and light.

ANIMAL CELLS

Unlike protozoa, animals are far too large to be put on a slide and examined under the microscope. Instead, we'll devote this chapter to looking at the smallest components of animal tissue— the cells. In a complex animal, every part and organ has its own unique type of cells. Let's start by looking at a few specialized cells of the human body.

CHEEK CELLS

Easy to obtain and examine are the cells that form a protective layer inside our cheeks. They are called *epithelial* cells. Like the similar cells that form the skin that covers our bodies, they are constantly worn off and replaced by other cells of the same type.

Gently scrape the inside of your cheek with the flat end of a toothpick. Be careful not to dig into your cheek. Mount the

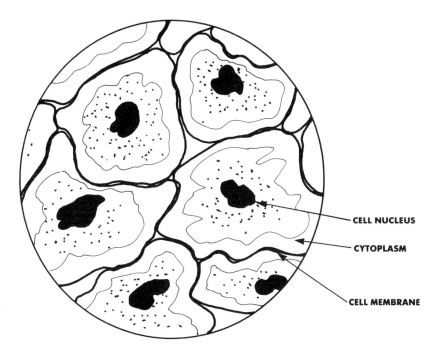

CELL NUCLEUS

CYTOPLASM

CELL MEMBRANE

Epithelial cells from the lining inside a person's cheek, magnified about 900×. The black dots are probably bacteria lying on the surface of the cells.

scrapings on a clean, dry slide. Add a drop of water and a cover slip. When you examine the slide under low power you will see many clusters or sheets of irregularly shaped cells. Epithelial cells are attached to one another to form a protective lining and usually come off the cheek in large masses.

Focusing on one particular cell, you should be able to see the *nucleus,* a small spherical body in the center. The nucleus contains the *chromosomes,* or hereditary material of the cell. Surrounding the nucleus is the *cytoplasm,* and the entire cell is covered by a *cell membrane.* You will notice that the cells have little depth and are, in fact, quite flat.

Epithelial cells tend to look pale and transparent under the microscope. If you find it hard to pick out any definite structure, you will get a much clearer picture of the cells by staining them with tincture of iodine.

Before you do this, read the section called "Using Stains for Better Visibility" at the end of Chapter 5. After you have taken all the necessary precautions, add a drop of iodine to the epithelial cells on the slide. You need only touch the applicator to the side of the slide to see the stain drawn under the cover slip. After a few minutes, add a drop or two of water to rinse off the stain. Hold the slide over some paper towels while you are doing this. Then place the slide under the microscope.

The cell nuclei will now be dark brown and far more prominent than before. You can sometimes see bacteria on the surface of the cells. When stained, bacteria look like small dark spots or rods spread at random over the cell.

BLOOD CELLS

Another group of cells exciting to see and not difficult to obtain are blood cells. Ask an adult to help you draw a drop of blood from your fingertip by pricking it with a sharp, sterilized needle. Before you start, sterilize the needle by passing the tip through a flame. Discard the needle after using it. To avoid infection, clean your finger with an alcohol solution before and after you use the needle.

Place the drop of blood squeezed from your finger near the end of a clean slide. Then take another slide and lower it until it touches the first slide at an angle of about 45 degrees. Move it along the first slide until it just touches the drop of blood and the blood spreads along its edge. Now push the spreader slide quickly back again toward the opposite end of the slide, so that it draws a film of blood behind it. This should produce a

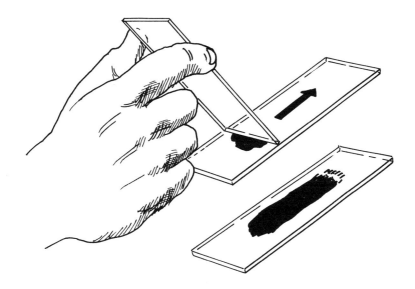

To prepare a blood smear, move the top slide quickly and lightly, so that the blood is pulled behind it and the cells are not crushed.

thin smear without damaging the cells.

Make sure that the smear is even and that there are no thick blotches. The smear should be thin enough to appear pale yellow in color rather than red. Let the smear dry in air. Do not add a cover slip. When you examine the slide you will see large numbers of red blood cells, or *erythrocytes* (*erythro-* means red). If you have found an area of the slide that is not too densely packed, you will be able to examine individual red blood cells. They are shaped like doughnuts with concave, or pushed in, centers. Blood contains enormous numbers of erythrocytes. Each milliliter (1 milliliter = one thousandth of a liter) holds about 5 million red blood cells. The red blood cells carry oxygen from the lungs to the tissues and are responsible for the blood's bright red color.

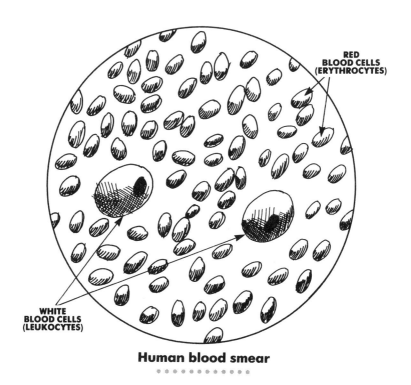

WHITE
BLOOD CELLS
(LEUKOCYTES)

Human blood smear

Unlike a cheek cell, a red blood cell has no nucleus. Because of this it can't reproduce itself and simply wears out and disintegrates after about 120 days (4 months).

In addition to the red blood cells, a few white blood cells should be visible. The white blood cells, or *leukocytes,* are much larger than the red blood cells. In spite of their name, they are not really white, but colorless. There are more than five hundred red blood cells for every white blood cell, so you may have to search several areas of the slide to locate one. White blood cells are a very important part of the body's defense against foreign material, such as bacteria.

If you add a few drops of methylene blue to the smear,

you will see that unlike the red blood cells, the white blood cells have a nucleus.

A blood smear is a good specimen to make into a permanent slide. Follow the directions for permanent mounts in Chapter 4. Before you start, make sure the blood specimen is completely dry.

MUSCLE CELLS

Cuts of uncooked red meat, right from your refrigerator, are an excellent source of muscle cells. Slice a sliver as thin as you can make it from a raw roast or a steak and place it on a slide. You can use a pair of sharp knives or needles to spread the meat out as much as possible. Add a drop of a stain, such as methylene blue or iodine, to darken the cell nuclei and make them easier to see.

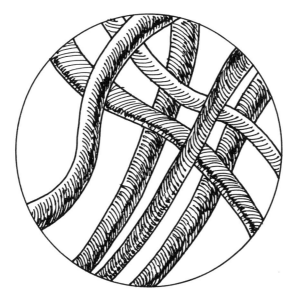

Muscle cells magnified about 180×. The fine cross lines, or *striations*, show that these are voluntary muscle cells.

Muscle cells are very long and look like bundles of fibers. Each cell has many nuclei. Running across each cell you will see stripes that form a banding pattern. These stripes are really tiny fibers in the cell that give the muscle its ability to contract and move various parts of the body. This kind of *striated* tissue is called a voluntary muscle cell because the mind can consciously will it to contract.

Some muscles can't be consciously controlled. The muscles in the stomach or the heart, for example, function automatically. These involuntary muscle cells are called smooth muscle cells because they lack the striations found in voluntary muscles.

To see smooth cells, get a butcher at your local market to save you some small pieces of animal intestine or heart. Under the microscope, the cells will look much smaller than the large, fiberlike voluntary muscle cells. They are shaped somewhat like spindles. If you use a stain such as iodine or red ink, you should be able to see the single nucleus that each cell contains right in the middle of the cell.

You might experiment with other types of animal parts such as liver or kidneys. The white elastic tissue called cartilage, found at the end of a chicken bone, is also an excellent specimen source. If you carefully cut a thin slice of cartilage with a razor blade or sharp knife and then add a drop of a stain, such as iodine, you can see many irregularly shaped cartilage cells and their nuclei.

8

INTRODUCING INSECTS

The insect world gives the microscopist an almost endless supply of fascinating specimens. Some insects are small enough to be seen in their entirety under the microscope. Mostly, however, you will have to examine individual parts, such as a wing or a stinger. It's not always necessary to hunt and kill an insect for examination. Look around the window ledges of your house, in a garden, or in a park, and you may be able to find flies, beetles, butterflies, and spiders that are already dead.

If you do have to kill an insect you'll want to do it as quickly and humanely as possible. A good way to do this is to place the insect in a jar with some cotton that has been soaked in household ammonia. Cover the jar and seal it. Work quickly to avoid breathing the vapors. After the insect is dead, remove it from the jar with a pair of tweezers and prepare it for mounting.

INSECT LEGS

An insect readily available everywhere is the common housefly. Like all insects, flies have six legs. You can detach one leg of a dead fly with a sharp pair of scissors and examine it under the microscope. Note that the leg is hairy and divided into five main parts. At the end of the foot there are small claws surrounding a soft cushionlike pad with numerous fine, sticky hairs that enable the fly to walk on a wall or ceiling.

You can examine the legs of other insects, such as grasshoppers, bees, ants, beetles, and butterflies. The rear legs of grasshoppers are very powerful, permitting them to make amazing long-distance leaps. Beetles that dig under the ground have very wide, powerful front legs. Butterflies have very poorly developed legs, since they spend most of their time in the air.

INSECT ANTENNAE

The antennae of insects are sometimes referred to as "feelers" and compared to a small radar instrument that permits the insect to sense its surroundings. In fact, while some insects feel with their antennae, others can smell and even hear with them. Watch a live insect closely and you'll often see it busy cleaning its antennae either with its mouth or with its legs.

Under the microscope you can see that the insect's two antennae are attached somewhere near the top of its head. The antennae usually have many segments so that they are flexible and can bend easily. Every type of insect has its own distinctive set of antennae. Some may look like two large feathers, while others look as if they were made of little cylinders linked together in a necklace.

If you examine the head of a mosquito and see that its antennae look like threads, you are looking at a female. If the antennae look like plumes, you have found a male. The male

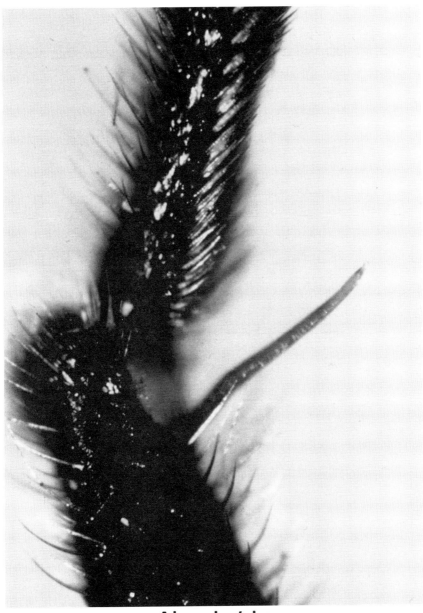

A honeybee's leg

mosquito uses these sensitive featherlike sense organs to listen for the presence of a female.

The moth is another insect that has very large and impressive antennae. Seen under the microscope, they may remind you of a bird's feathers.

INSECT WINGS

Examine the insect's wings. Some insects, like the fly, have two wings. Others, like the butterfly, have four wings—two large ones in front, and two smaller ones in the rear. Under the microscope you can clearly see the veinlike structure that strengthens the wing, as well as the hairs or scales that cover many wings. The wing of a housefly, for example, is almost as transparent as glass and dotted with sharp spike-like hairs. The wings of butterflies and moths are covered with dustlike scales that create wonderful colors and patterns. Compare the wings of different insects. Which insects have scales and which have hairs?

INSECT EYES

Study the eyes of the insects you have collected. You will find them at each side of the insect's head. The large oval eyes are made up of thousands of smaller eyes, each one contributing its own image to the insect's vision. The bulge of these compound eyes enables some insects to see what is going on all around them.

MORE ADVENTURES

The mouths of insects are also quite fascinating. Some have jawlike mandibles for chewing and grinding food, while others have a *proboscis* for sucking up food. The proboscis of butterflies is particularly impressive. When it is not extended, it lies coiled up in the form of a spiral under the butterfly's head.

A butterfly's wing

63

Look for the proboscis in mosquitoes. You will see it as an impressive tubelike structure that lies between the antennae. The female mosquito uses her proboscis to pierce the skin of her victim and suck out blood. The male's proboscis, though, is not strong enough to penetrate skin, and male mosquitoes suck their food from plants.

Spiders, too, are well worth examining. Spiders are not insects. Even without the microscope you can see that spiders have eight legs rather than an insect's six and that their bodies are divided into two parts while the bodies of insects are divided into three.

At back of the spider's abdomen are six small organs called the spinnerets. Each consists of many tubes that emit a sticky liquid. As soon as the liquid comes in contact with the air it hardens into a silky thread, which is the material for the spider's marvelous webs.

As you have seen, insects for microscopic study don't need to be rare or hard to collect. A walk in the woods or a stroll in the park can provide many specimens for further adventures with the microscope.

GLOSSARY

ACHROMATIC LENS
A lens made of a combination of different types of glass to prevent color distortions.

ALGAE
A group of chlorophyll-containing plants found in both salt water and fresh water as well as on land. Some are microscopically small, others may measure hundreds of feet in length. Certain algae are capable of independent motion.

AMEBA
A microscopic one-celled animal that continuously changes shape as it moves and engulfs food.

ANATOMY
The structure of animals and plants, or the science that studies those structures.

ANTENNAE

Appendages for sensing the environment that grow in pairs on the heads of insects, spiders, and other arthropods.

ANTHER

Part of the reproductive organs of flowers, baglike structures that hold pollen. They are located at the end of the filament of the stamen.

ANTIBIOTIC

Any chemical substance made from microbial products and used, as in medicine, to destroy microorganisms or inhibit their growth.

CARTILAGE

A firm, elastic, translucent substance that acts as structural connective tissue in animals and humans.

CAPILLARY ACTION

The principle by which thin channels enable water to travel upward against the force of gravity.

CILIA

Hairlike appendages on certain cells, sometimes used as a means of locomotion.

CHROMATIC ABERRATION

A lens defect that causes images to become blurred and ringed with colors.

CHROMOSOME

One of a set of threadlike formations in the cell nucleus.

Chromosomes carry the genes that hold the hereditary information of the cell.

Compound Microscope
A microscope that uses two lenses for double magnification.

Cytoplasm
All the material inside a cell, except the nucleus.

Depth of Focus
The range of distances that are simultaneously in focus.

Diaphragm
On a microscope, a plate located under the stage, with an adjustable opening for regulating the amount of light that falls on the slide.

Diatoms
Microscopic marine or fresh-water algae whose mineral content gives them a brittle, glittering texture.

Epithelial Cells
The cells of any tissue lining the outer or inner parts of the body, such as the skin or the mucous membranes.

Erythrocytes
The red blood cells that carry oxygen to the tissues of the body and return carbon dioxide to the respiratory organs.

Euglena
A group of single-celled algae, sometimes classified as animals because of their ability to move about on their own.

EUPARAL
A clear synthetic mounting material used for making permanent slides.

FLAGELLATES
Protozoa that move by means of flagella.

FLAGELLUM
A whiplike appendage on certain cells, used as a means of locomotion (plural: flagella).

FOCAL LENGTH
The distance between a lens and its focal point.

FOCAL POINT
The point at which a lens causes light rays to condense; the point at which an image forms.

FUNGUS
A plant that has no true stem, roots, or leaves; lacks chlorophyll; and feeds either as a parasite on living hosts or on decaying organic matter (plural: fungi).

LEUKOCYTE
A type of white blood cell.

MANDIBLE
A jawlike biting organ in insects and spiders.

MICROBE
A microscopic organism belonging either to the plant or the animal kingdom.

Microorganism
Any life form of microscopic size.

Mold
Minute fungi that form on animal or vegetable matter.

Nucleus
In cells, the structure that contains the chromosomes.

Objective Lens
The lower of the two lenses in a compound microscope.

Ocular Lens
The eyepiece, or upper lens, in a compound microscope.

Ovule
An egg cell formed in the female organ of a flower.

Paramecium
A freshwater protozoan shaped like the sole of a shoe and propelled by cilia.

Parasite
An organism that lives by feeding on a plant or animal host.

Pistil
The female sex organ of a flower.

Pollen
A yellowish powder that is the fertilizing element of flowers.

PROBOSCIS

The long, protruding mouth parts of certain insects.

PROTOZOA

One-celled organisms that are the simplest of all animals (singular: protozoan).

PSEUDOPOD

A projection of the body sent out by a certain group of microbes as a means of locomotion; the rest of the cell body follows by slowly oozing into the projection.

SIMPLE MICROSCOPE

A microscope containing only one lens, essentially a magnifying glass.

SMOOTH MUSCLE CELLS

Cells of the involuntary muscles, which lack the striations of other types of muscle tissue.

SPIROGYRA

Fresh-water algae that show spiral bands of green chlorophyll.

SPINNERETS

In spiders, the three pairs of spinning organs located at the end of the abdomen. They spin the silky thread for the web.

SPORES

In nonflowering plants such as ferns and mosses, the reproductive bodies that ripen, drop from the plant, and create new plants where they fall.

SPOROZOA

A group of spore-forming protozoa all of which are parasites. They are small and have no organs of locomotion in the adult stage.

STAMEN

The pollen-bearing reproductive organ of flowers. It consists of the filament and the anther.

STRIATED MUSCLE CELLS

Cells that make up the voluntary or consciously controlled muscles. They show alternating light and dark stripes under the microscope.

YEAST

Any one of a group of single-celled fungi. Some yeasts can cause infections, but others are useful in making bread, wine and beer.

SCIENTIFIC SUPPLY HOUSES

The following companies are excellent sources of microscopes and accessories, prepared microscopic slides, mounting fluids, and chemical stains. From some of these companies you can also purchase videocassettes showing techniques for handling the microscope and computer software simulating microscope techniques, for use with both IBM-compatible and Apple computers.

Carolina Biological Supply Co.
2700 York Road
Burlington, NC 27215

1-800-334-5551

Central Scientific Company
11222 Melrose Avenue
Franklin Park, IL 60131

1-800-262-3620

Edmund Scientific Co.
101 E. Gloucester Pike
Barrington, NJ 08007

1-609-573-6250

Fisher-EMD
4901 W. Le Moyne Street
Chicago, IL 60651

1-800-621-4769

Frey Scientific Company
905 Hickory Lane
Mansfield, OH 44905

1-800-225-FREY

Sargent-Welch
7300 North Linder Avenue
P.O. Box 1026
Skokie, IL 60077

1-800-727-4368

For Microscopes Only

Buehler Ltd.
41 Waukegan Road
P.O. Box 1
Lake Bluff, IL 60044

Nikon Inc.
623 Stewart Avenue
Garden City, NY 11530

Olympus Corporation
4 Nevada Drive
Lake Success, NY 11042

Reichert-Jung
Cambridge Instruments Inc.
P.O. Box 123
Buffalo, NY 14240

Warner Lambert Technologies, Inc.
P.O. Box 123
Buffalo, NY 14240

For Service, Cleaning, Repair of New and Reconditioned Instruments

Mel Sobel Microscopes, Ltd.
11 Favorite Lane
Jericho, NY 11753

1-516-935-7794

INDEX

ABOUT
THE AUTHORS

Albert and Eve Stwertka often work together on books about science and the environment. Albert, whose field is atomic physics, heads the math and science department of the Federal Maritime Academy, Kings Point. Eve is an English professor at the State University of New York at Farmingdale. They have written on such topics as industrial pollution, population, genetic engineering, and medical computers.